COACH YOURSELF BETTER, FAST

THE SPEED STORYTELLING TOOLKIT

Based on *Exposure* by Felicity Cowie

First published in Great Britain by Practical Inspiration Publishing, 2025

© Felicity Cowie and Practical Inspiration Publishing, 2025

The moral rights of the author have been asserted.

ISBN 9781788607476   (paperback)
      9781788607483   (epub)
      9781788607490   (Kindle)

All rights reserved. This book, or any portion thereof, may not be reproduced without the express written permission of the publisher.

Every effort has been made to trace copyright holders and to obtain their permission for the use of copyright material. The publisher apologizes for any errors or omissions and would be grateful if notified of any corrections that should be incorporated in future reprints or editions of this book.

EU GPSR representative: LOGOS EUROPE, 9 rue Nicolas Poussin, LA ROCHELLE 17000, France Contact@logoseurope.eu

Want to bulk-buy copies of this book for your team and colleagues? We can customize the content and co-brand *The Speed Storytelling Toolkit* to suit your business's needs.

Please email info@practicalinspiration.com for more details.

Contents

Series introduction v

Introduction 1

Day 1: Hero (who) 7

Day 2: Action (what) 13

Day 3: Setting (where) 19

Day 4: Timeline (when) 25

Day 5: Process (how) 31

Day 6: Motivation (why) 39

Day 7: Assembly (bringing it all together) 47

Day 8: Engagement 53

Day 9: Collaboration 59

Day 10: Momentum 67

Conclusion 75

50 Mighty Words® framework 77

One story, many business uses: adapting your speed storytelling blocks 79

Team-building: speed storytelling together 81

Series introduction

Welcome to *6-Minute Smarts*!

This is a series of very short books with one simple purpose: to introduce you to ideas that can make life and work better, and to give you time and space to think about how those ideas might apply to your life and work.

Each book introduces you to ten powerful ideas, but ideas on their own are useless – that's why each idea is followed by self-coaching questions to help you work out the 'so what?' for you in just six minutes of exploratory writing. What's exploratory writing? It's the kind of writing you do just for yourself, fast and free, without worrying what anyone else thinks. It's not just about getting ideas out of your head and onto paper where you can see them, it's about finding new connections and insights as you write. This is where the magic happens.

Find out more...

Introduction

What do you feel when someone says 'Let me tell you a story'? Personally, I feel delighted – if I'm in Nashville at a sold-out, intimate songwriter's circle in an iconic venue, enjoying the holiday of a lifetime. But if I'm up against a work deadline, needing quick answers or eager to wrap up a meeting to get to the next one, hearing those words can drive me crazy. So, why is storytelling becoming such a big deal at work? And, more importantly, how can it help you?

The answer lies in its ability to make sharing information *easier*, *quicker* and *more compelling* for both you and your audience.

Easier

Think about how much easier it is to remember the colours of the rainbow if you know the song 'I can sing a rainbow'. There's substantial research showing that our brains naturally search for patterns and meaning when presented with new information. Good stories do some of that work for us – they organize information, link ideas in sequence and make it easier to understand, remember and, crucially, share.

This isn't a modern phenomenon; it's deeply ingrained. Throughout human history, people have passed on vital information – warnings, survival tips and cultural lessons – through storytelling. Our brains have evolved to pay attention to shared stories because they carry important insights. Think about how uncomfortable it feels to be 'the last to know' about any shared news in your work or social circles.

Quicker

Imagine how productive meetings could be if everyone distilled key points into a 50-word introduction. What if, when it's your turn to speak, your idea or project is instantly understood – or at least understood enough to spark meaningful discussion? What if, after a meeting, there was a shared understanding that could be easily conveyed to others? That's the power of speed storytelling.

Introduction

More compelling

We're wired to process new information by running it through six key questions: Who? What? Where? When? How? Why? Think of these as human algorithms, constantly sorting and evaluating incoming data. When you build a story using these six blocks and present it in around 50 words, you're not just relaying information – you're satisfying the natural curiosity algorithms we all rely on. It's like giving the brain a clear answer to what it's instinctively searching for, making the information instantly more engaging and memorable.

For example, imagine presenting a new product at a team meeting. Instead of diving straight into technical specs, you could start with a 50-word speed story:

> Our new software, Taskd, helps remote teams collaborate more effectively by providing real-time project updates and automatic task reminders. It's been developed using insights from three years of user feedback, incorporating AI to streamline workflows. Now teams can stay on track without missing a beat.

In just a few sentences, you've covered the who (Taskd), what (helps teams collaborate), where (remote teams), when (based on three years of feedback), how (AI and real-time updates) and why (to stay on track). This approach instantly satisfies the audience's mental algorithms and sets the stage for a deeper conversation. It's also inclusive – no one at the meeting is left guessing what's being discussed.

How to use this book

By the end of this book, you'll be able to tell a complete story in around 50 words using a process that's quick and effective. You'll practise with the six fundamental building blocks: who, what, where, when, how and why. Over ten days, you'll focus on each block to understand its role and then put them together to build your first speed story.

Each chapter starts with a three-minute read, followed by a six-minute exercise – because this is a *6-Minute Smarts* book! By investing just ten minutes a day, you'll develop a storytelling process that's agile enough for everyday business scenarios, helping you to spark interest, start conversations and inspire action.

Introduction

As you progress, you'll see how these elements combine to form a cohesive, impactful story. By Day 7, you'll assemble all the blocks into your own powerful tool for business communication. The remaining chapters will guide you on how to adapt your new storytelling skills for different contexts, ensuring that your stories are always clear, engaging and effective.

Why speed storytelling matters

This book is based on my award-winning work *Exposure*, which shares insights from my years as a *BBC News* and *Panorama* journalist, revealing how newsrooms tell stories at speed, how businesses can best engage with the media and the lessons I've learned from handling both sides of around 100,000 story pitches.

Readers of *Exposure* consistently value its practical approach to clear, concise storytelling, especially for identifying and communicating a business's core story quickly. Reviews highlight how the tools helped people engage more effectively – not just with journalists, but also within their organizations for internal communications, stakeholder management and business transformation. Many found that mastering these skills gave them the confidence to articulate their visions and drive action.

This book strips everything else away to focus solely on speed storytelling, offering you a clear, practical process to build stories that give you clarity, boost your confidence and inspire others to take positive, timely action. I'm sharing with you the exact framework I used to navigate my way through every pitch, breaking news story and major event – using these six essential story blocks.

Your story begins here

If you're ready to use a clear, practical and tested process to build stories that give you clarity, boost your confidence and inspire others to take positive and timely actions, then let's get started.

Day 1
Hero (who)

One of the biggest challenges in business storytelling is deciding who to focus your story on. Should it be your personal history and vision, the unique outcomes you deliver or your ideal client's needs? All of these considerations often lead to overcomplication, which can dilute your message.

The solution is much simpler than it seems. The focus should simply be on the name of the 'thing' you want others to know more about. It's a straightforward approach that's often overlooked, causing even great stories to stumble right from the start.

The hero's identity

Let's explore an example. Eva is the founder of GrowBot, a tech company that has developed a pioneering robotic system to help farmers manage their crops more efficiently. While Eva's back story is fascinating, her technology is impressive and the benefits she offers farmers are significant, the true focus of her business story must be GrowBot itself. Ultimately, Eva's goal is to generate interest in GrowBot so it can thrive. GrowBot is the hero of the story. Even if Eva wins Entrepreneur of the Year, revolutionizes farming worldwide or solves every farmer's problem, none of these achievements matter if GrowBot isn't at the heart of her narrative.

Even when Eva introduces herself as 'Eva, the founder of GrowBot', the hero remains GrowBot. She is providing context and positioning herself as a guide to the main story, but the spotlight should still be on what GrowBot does, why it matters and the impact it delivers. By consistently positioning GrowBot as the hero, she helps her audience focus on the value that GrowBot brings to the world.

Hero (who)

Personalizing the hero

Now, think about yourself and what drew you to the idea of developing speed storytelling for your own work. What do you want others to know about? Is it a business, like Eva's, that you want to amplify? Or perhaps a new project or system at work that needs adoption? Regardless of the scenario, the 'thing' you want others to know more about is your hero.

Naming your hero

What if your 'thing' doesn't have a name yet? Make naming it a priority. If you don't, others will label it for you, and you may lose control over the narrative. This ties into the concept of 'anchoring bias', as described by Amos Tversky and Daniel Kahneman. Essentially, people rely heavily on the first piece of information they're given about any new subject and interpret subsequent details from that initial anchor. Ideally, give your 'thing' a name that clearly conveys what it does – like 'GrowBot'.

But if you're stuck with something more generic, such as 'Project Change', don't worry. The key is to use your chosen name consistently so that each time it appears, people are ready to hear more of the story.

So what? Over to you...

1. What is the name of your 'thing' – who is the hero of your business story? If you haven't named it yet, brainstorm some ideas and figure out how to get it approved, if needed, as soon as possible.

Hero (who)

2. Is your business name consistently used across all communications? Make a list of key places where your business name appears (e.g. website, presentations, social media). Are there any areas where it's missing, or could it be featured more prominently?

3. Do you introduce your business name early and clearly, and say it comfortably? Reflect on how you present your business in various situations (e.g. meetings, emails). Are you introducing the name right from the start, or are you assuming people will infer it from your logo? Practise using the name in different contexts to ensure it feels natural and confident.

Day 2
Action (what)

Yesterday, you discovered how much easier it is to tell a story once you've identified who the focus should be on – essentially, the 'thing' you want others to know about, whether that's your business, project or initiative. You also gave it a name, just as you would for the hero of a book or film.

This works because heroes drive action. Today, we'll zero in on the main action your hero – your business or project – is taking and distil it into as few words as possible.

Finding the right balance

The trick here is to find the balance between being too general and too detailed. Imagine you're at a social event and the inevitable 'So, what do you do?' question comes up. Our brains are wired to seek context and understanding, so this question is a natural shortcut to make sense of new information. Here's how three different people might respond:

- **Person 1:** 'I'm making the world a better place.'
- **Person 2:** 'I engineer synergistic solutions to optimize cross-functional innovation ecosystems within the adaptive meshwork of post-digital transformation landscapes.'
- **Person 3:** 'I've created a robot that helps farmers manage their crops better.'

Now, imagine you're all heading to a table for a two-hour dinner. Who are you most likely to sit next to?

Person 2 probably won't be your first choice. Unless you share their specific expertise, you'd likely struggle to follow the conversation – and two hours is a long time to feel lost.

Person 1 is a gamble. 'Making the world a better place' sounds intriguing, but it could be anything from feeding the hungry to designing luxury yachts. You'd have to ask more questions to figure out whether the conversation is worth pursuing. Worst

Action (what)

case, they might end up talking about synergistic solutions after all.

Person 3 seems like the safest bet. Even if you don't know much about robots or farming, there's enough context to keep the conversation interesting – and who doesn't love robots? Plus, this person has shown they can communicate like a fellow human, so you might actually learn something.

Clarifying your action

Today's goal is to help you strike that balance when describing what your own hero is doing. Your audience needs enough context to grasp what action your business or project is taking, but without being overwhelmed by jargon or left in the dark with vague statements.

Clarity encourages people to engage further and explore your story. You want your 'what' to provide enough insight to spark curiosity and invite more conversation. Your hero takes action – now it's time to articulate that action clearly.

So what? Over to you…

1. What does your hero do? List all the different things your business or project does. Then, look for a common theme or goal. Imagine your business as a box set – what is the overall story arc that connects all the episodes?

Action (what)

2. Is your description simple and clear enough for anyone to understand quickly? Think about the social event scenario again. Would your answer make someone want to keep the conversation going? If not, simplify it and avoid acronyms, buzzwords or jargon.

3. Does the 'what' align with your core business goals? Cross-check your description with your main objectives. Make sure it reflects what you want your business to be known for, not just what's important to your current top client.

Day 3
Setting (where)

By now, you've named the hero of your speed story and defined the main action they're taking. Congratulations – give yourself a small cheer! Now, it's time to make your story even more compelling by anchoring the action in context, using two powerful reference points: space and time.

Humans instinctively trust the categories of space and time. From early humans navigating landscapes and seasons to today's business focus on location data and quarterly results, these elements help us organize and make sense of the world. By grounding your story in a clear context, you tap into these trusted instincts, making your narrative more engaging, relatable and memorable.

Defining the setting

The setting answers the question of where your story unfolds. Think back to GrowBot, our example from Day 1. GrowBot is based at founder Eva's farm in Somerset, but the setting doesn't have to be a specific location. It could be a sector, such as farming, health care or education, or even a problem-solving activity, like parking a tractor safely. The key is to establish the context where your hero operates and where the action takes place.

If what you do is particularly pioneering, you can still leverage what is familiar by framing your story in terms of the problem it solves. For example, you could say your solution was invented to address challenges faced while managing a bank, designing software or writing a book. This approach helps people connect with your story, even if they're not familiar with your specific product or service.

A well-defined setting adds depth, making your story feel grounded. It helps your audience understand where your business or project fits into their world. Whether the setting is a place, a digital space, a sector or a problem-solving context, it creates a connection that draws your audience into the narrative, allowing them to visualize where the

Setting (where)

action happens. This connection helps them relate to your story and see its relevance to their own lives.

You don't need to use many words to establish a setting, because even a brief description can evoke an image or idea. For example, saying 'GrowBot helps farmers manage irrigation' can suggest the challenge of dry farmland, while 'Project Change will move our solutions into the cloud' hints at the vast possibilities of cloud technology. A few well-chosen words can effectively provide context, making it easier for your audience to connect with the story.

 So what? Over to you…

1. Does the setting clearly establish where your business operates? Identify whether it's a physical, digital or conceptual space, and ensure the audience can quickly grasp this.

2. Are you leveraging any familiar locations, industries, markets or problems? Think of where your business fits within larger, well-known contexts. This helps people understand and validate what you do more quickly.

Setting (where)

3. Is this setting specific enough to provide context but broad enough to apply across your activities? Make sure the 'where' supports all your business operations and activities while still giving your audience a fast, clear picture.

Day 4
Timeline (when)

In my experience, when people are presented with a new business idea or change project, they often react like journalists assessing a potential news story. Most are risk-averse – reluctant to be the first to invest time or resources into something new. Yet, paradoxically, they quickly become frustrated if they feel left out once the initiative gains momentum.

In the business world, it's common to hear 'But this is how we've always done it', followed shortly after by 'We needed to know about this sooner so we could have factored it in.' This tension arises because people's perception of time is highly subjective – either they don't see the need for immediate change or they regret missing out once progress becomes evident. It creates a challenge when you need others to prioritize your timeline.

Addressing resistance

The good news is that our perceptions of time, risk and credibility are deeply linked. When you use speed storytelling, you can tap into the inherent trust people place in time to reduce perceived risks and build credibility faster.

So, how do you achieve this with just a few words?

Think about the hero's experience. Let's revisit our GrowBot example. Imagine GrowBot was born out of founder Eva's 20 years of farming experience and a partnership with a university robotics lab. Or consider Project Change, which addresses trends identified over five years of employee and client feedback. Both examples show that the hero brings accumulated experience and insights to the table. It's not just the founder's or project leader's background that adds depth; reputable partnerships, long-term data collection or industry-specific knowledge also contribute to building a story's credibility.

The emphasis is often placed on novelty, but that overlooks the fact that working with novelty can be

Timeline (when)

challenging. Fresh ideas generate initial excitement, but as implementation gets tough, the familiar – 'business as usual' – often reclaims the energy. By grounding your story in elements that reflect time and reliability, you help maintain momentum even as enthusiasm fluctuates.

There's a belief that snappy headlines and catchy press releases are what draw journalists to a story. That's not quite right. When I sifted through thousands of emails on the main planning desk at the BBC, what often caught my eye was the brief description of the organization or project. I needed to understand who the source was before investing my time. Journalists, like busy professionals, value familiarity and credibility – especially when time is limited.

Incorporating time into your storytelling builds trust. Emphasizing long-term experience, reputable collaborations or data-driven insights allows your audience to engage with your narrative confidently, without hesitation.

So what? Over to you...

1. What past experiences or partnerships can I leverage to demonstrate credibility for my project? Identify collaborations, long-term experience or industry-specific insights that can strengthen your message.

Timeline (when)

2. Am I clearly communicating the time frame over which insights or knowledge were gathered? Articulate the history behind your project in a few words. For example, 'developed over a decade of research' or 'based on five years of feedback'.

3. Is there anything familiar I can connect my idea to that people already trust? If you're struggling, connect your story to a past success or established context. For instance: 'Project Change builds on the success of Project Gold, which doubled customer engagement.'

Day 5
Process (how)

You might be wondering why we've made it to Day 5 – halfway through our journey – without focusing on how something is or will be achieved. The reason is simple: the 'how' involves a deeper level of detail, and it's crucial to lay a strong foundation with the previous steps before diving into it. Doing so not only prepares your audience but also brings you clarity on what matters most.

Think of a film, book or song you love. There's always an introduction that helps you get to know the hero and understand what's at stake. The rest of the story is about how the hero tackles those stakes. By the time the how is revealed, you're already invested and everything falls into place.

Now, imagine missing the first ten minutes of a film. You'd likely struggle to follow the unfolding action, constantly trying to catch up on who the hero is and what they're trying to achieve. Even if you know the lead actor and the general plot, coming in mid-scene can still be disorienting. Your brain might even question, 'Wait, wasn't Zendaya supposed to be in this? Am I in the right cinema?'

Breaking down the how

In speed storytelling, the how is where you could lose people if you get bogged down in too much detail too soon. Your goal is to build enough interest that your audience starts asking 'But how does it work? Can you tell me more?' This curiosity primes them to be more receptive to the how when you finally reveal it.

To make it manageable, consider breaking the how into three parts:

1. **The method:** Explain the primary approach or technique that defines your how. Think of this as the headline how – the thing that's at the core of what you do. For GrowBot, it might be: 'The robot uses a combination of sensor technology, AI-driven analytics and automated systems.' For a mental health app,

Process (how)

it might be: 'We use cognitive behavioural techniques and guided meditations to help users manage stress.' The method should be clear and easily understandable.

2. **The process:** This is where you outline the key steps involved in your how. It's not about getting into the weeds, but about giving enough structure that people can see how the method is put into action. For GrowBot, this might involve steps like 'detect soil moisture levels', 'analyse weather patterns' and 'automatically adjust irrigation schedules'. The process helps your audience visualize the journey your hero takes to achieve the desired outcome.

3. **The flexibility:** Here, you identify what can be adapted or tailored based on feedback or evolving needs. This is the part of your how that invites collaboration or future improvements. For example, Eva might say: 'We're continuously refining GrowBot's software based on user feedback to improve accuracy.' In the case of Project Change, it could be: 'The frequency of updates will be adjusted based on team feedback to ensure we're delivering value without overwhelming staff.'

By breaking the how into these three parts, you're providing a structured explanation that's both grounded and adaptable. It also allows your audience to understand the essential processes while seeing where there's room for growth and involvement.

You may not include all three in your speed story – you might just pick one aspect that is integral to everything, such as a specific process or a patented technology. But this approach helps you unpack the how in a way that adds depth and clarity.

If this has got you thinking that the how isn't actually very clear yet and you'd like to discuss it with your team, don't worry. There's a team-building exercise later in the book specifically designed to help you and your team clarify your how together.

So what? Over to you...

1. What is your headline 'how' – the main method you use? Identify the core approach or technique that defines your how in one concise statement.

2. What are the key steps in your process? List the primary actions or steps involved in putting your method into practice. Keep it simple.

Process (how)

3. Which parts of your how are open to change or development? Determine where there's room for flexibility, feedback or future growth. Frame these areas as opportunities for collaboration.

Day 6
Motivation (why)

The 'why' often gets all the glory in business storytelling, viewed as the heart of the story that connects with your audience. But here's the crucial point: the why only resonates effectively when it follows a clear who, what, where, when and how. Without this foundation, the why can feel unconvincing or vague.

Inviting curiosity

Think back to the dinner party example from Day 2. The person who vaguely claimed they were 'changing the world' didn't offer enough context to be the most engaging choice of dinner companion. In contrast, the person who provided specific details about who they were and what they did struck the right balance, naturally making you curious about their why.

Grounding the why

The why gains power when it's grounded in facts and context. Use past experiences, partnerships or evidence to give it weight. For instance, 'Our initiative is backed by 20 years of industry experience and collaboration with leading experts' is more compelling than a generic statement like 'We just believe it's the right thing to do.' This approach not only adds credibility but also makes the story relatable.

The why as an invitation

Think about when someone tells you what they do at a party. If they've provided enough context, the most natural response might be 'How did you get into that?' – which is essentially asking 'Why are you doing it?' The why serves as an invitation to engage, prompting curiosity and opening the door to deeper conversations.

Motivation (why)

Making the why meaningful

When the why is positioned well, it creates a strong connection. In my experience training businesses in speed storytelling, the why stands out when it feels like a natural continuation of the other story elements. Once people understand what GrowBot is and how it works, Eva's why – to help struggling farms through better technology – becomes compelling because it's tied to something concrete. Similarly, Project Change's why – to build a more adaptable culture – resonates when the what (streamlined communication) is already clear.

Avoiding generic statements

Avoid generic 'why' statements. In business, these are often used as placeholders when deeper consensus is difficult. For example, 'We want to keep customers at the heart of everything we do' may sound good, but it doesn't convey the true urgency if the real reason for change is that the business is falling behind competitors. Being transparent helps build trust more effectively than vague phrases.

Respecting confidentiality

Sometimes, confidentiality limits how much can be shared. For instance, if a director takes leave for health reasons, the why may be communicated as: 'Our colleague is taking time away for personal reasons, and we fully support them. The Chief Operations Officer will manage the team during this period.' This explanation maintains transparency while respecting privacy.

Storytelling as a process

The why should emerge naturally from the other story blocks. The most impactful why statements add depth by drawing on specific details. Instead of starting with a lofty why, integrate it into a well-structured story that prepares your audience for the motivation behind your business or project. This makes the why more than just a statement – it becomes an invitation for your audience to engage.

Motivation (why)

✏️ So what? Over to you…

1. Why is your hero (your business or project) doing what it does, and does this 'why' work for all your stakeholders? Think about the real motivations driving your business or project. Avoid buzzwords or clichés. Focus on the most significant problem your business aims to solve and why it matters. Then, consider if your why resonates across all stakeholders. If it doesn't, think about some 'sub-whys' that add an extra layer of detail for different groups while still aligning with your overall message.

2. Does your why fit naturally with the who, what, where and when? Go back to your earlier story blocks and check whether the why aligns seamlessly. Ensure it adds meaning to the existing context, rather than feeling detached or forced.

Motivation (why)

3. Is your why authentic? Practise saying your why out loud. Does it feel sincere and aligned with your values? Test it in different situations – such as sharing it with a colleague or someone outside your organization who you respect, or even with someone who might be sceptical. Notice whether it resonates each time.

Day 7
Assembly (bringing it all together)

Hurrah! You've now got all six building blocks for your story:

- **The hero:** who the story focuses on – your business or project
- **The action:** what action the hero is taking
- **The setting:** where the hero has an impact
- **The timeline:** when the hero gathered experience or connected to trends
- **The process:** how the hero can take action
- **The motivation:** why the hero is doing all of the above – the benefit

Speed Storytelling

Now, let's bring these blocks together to assemble your first speed story, which you can use to accelerate interest in your business or project.

GrowBot example: bringing it all together

Let's revisit GrowBot to demonstrate how to assemble your building blocks into a cohesive story:

- **Who:** GrowBot
- **What:** a robot designed to help farmers manage their crops more efficiently
- **Where:** used on farms struggling with irrigation
- **When:** built from founder Eva's experience as a farmer and her partnership with a university robotics lab
- **How:** uses sensor technology and AI to optimize crop management
- **Why:** to help farmers thrive despite current climate challenges, as Eva knows first-hand how hard this can be

Next, let's turn this into a story by making each section flow into the next with a few additional words. Here's how it works for GrowBot (I've italicized the added words for clarity):

Assembly (bringing it all together)

GrowBot *is* a robot designed to help farmers manage their crops more efficiently. *It's* used on farms struggling with irrigation *and* built from founder Eva's experience as a farmer and her partnership with a university robotics lab. *GrowBot* uses sensor technology and AI to optimize crop management. *It was created* to help farmers thrive despite current climate challenges.

How do you feel when you read this? Imagine receiving an email titled 'Introduction to GrowBot' and opening it to find this succinct summary instead of a link to a 67-slide presentation deck. Wouldn't that make a difference to your mood and interest level? Imagine if someone pinged you a diary invite for a meeting in ten minutes called 'GrowBot catch-up' and you found this email to brief yourself. How would you feel going into that meeting?

This may seem like a small detail, but it's powerful. The whole story is only 58 words. You want to keep it around 50 – any higher and you're getting too detailed; any lower and you might be too general or have skipped one of the blocks!

This concise storytelling approach forms the foundation of what I call my 50 **Mighty**

Words® system, and now you have it to use whenever you need it. Now, it's time to put it into action.

> ### ✏️ So what? Over to you...
>
> 1. What is your story? Go back through your self-coaching answers from previous days to bring your own words forward. Use these prompts: Who? What? Where? When? How? Why?

Assembly (bringing it all together)

2. Can you turn your answers into one paragraph of around 50 words? Put all these answers together and add any other words you need for flow.

3. Does it feel and sound engaging? Practise reading it aloud while thinking about how you might use it in an email or to answer the question: 'So, what are you working on right now?' Adjust as needed.

Day 8
Engagement

Now that you've mastered speed storytelling and crafted your own story through the self-coaching exercises, it's time to put it to the test. You've created a powerful tool – now let's use it to make a real-world impact!

The power of these stories lies in their ability to spark engagement, drive collaboration and build momentum. Over the next three days, you'll discover how to leverage your story to do just that. Let's dive in and see how far it can take you!

You may wonder why it was relatively straightforward to create a story using these specific blocks – who, what, where, when, how and why. These questions form the cornerstone of all journalism. During my training as a journalist, I learned to build every story from these fundamental elements. In my early days as a court reporter, tasked with navigating complex legal jargon and real human dramas, these questions served as my compass, helping me distil information quickly and effectively to meet tough deadlines.

While journalists are trained storytellers who have tested these blocks extensively, the reason they work is that they align with the way we all naturally process information. We continuously run these questions over incoming data – they act as our mental algorithms to categorize and evaluate information. When information is clearly organized, we can decide whether we want to engage further.

You may also have wondered why these stories are so short – around 50 words. Think of them as 'brain injections' delivering answers quickly. This brevity accelerates people's ability to engage with you. Short stories are highly flexible, easy to memorize and adaptable to different contexts. Whether inserted into bios or adjusted to fit character limits, the six blocks can be easily tailored. This flexibility encourages consistent use, which builds trust. Our brains are more receptive to new information when it's linked to something familiar – something we've already processed and accepted. By keeping your

Engagement

stories consistent, you reinforce familiarity and trust, making them even more effective.

Now that you understand how it all works and you've brought your audience to the brink of further engagement, the next crucial step is to show them how to take action – this is called a 'call to action'.

Your ultimate call to action might be 'meet my deadline' or 'buy my product', but it's far too early in the engagement process to ask for that directly, even if it's implied. We all know that when we get an email from a shop, no matter how clever, funny or intuitive, it's ultimately asking us to buy something.

At this stage, your call to action is simply 'come find out more for yourself'. You've made them aware that your 'shop' exists, and now you're opening the door, inviting them to look around on their own terms.

For example, Eva might end her GrowBot story with: 'If you'd like to know more, visit growbot.io to see how we're helping farmers thrive.' This addition is clear, specific and inviting.

Similarly, Project Change could conclude with: 'Come join us at the Town Hall meeting next Tuesday, where our Director of Transformation will share more about Project Change. We'll send the link around later for those who can't make it.'

This builds on the foundation your story has created by keeping the spark of engagement alive. The call to action is clear, specific and easy to act on – an inviting next step that encourages further conversation.

So what? Over to you…

1. What do you want your audience to do after hearing your story? Identify the specific action you want your audience to take. Is it visiting your website, attending an event or subscribing to a newsletter?

Engagement

2. Is your call to action clear, specific and easy to follow? Review your call to action to ensure it's simple and inviting. Would someone unfamiliar with your business understand what to do next?

3. How can you make your call to action more inviting and low-risk for your audience? Think about ways to reduce any potential hesitation. Can you make it more accessible by providing a link, inviting them to a free event or assuring them they can learn more on their own terms?

Day 9
Collaboration

Now that you've crystallized your work into enough words to visualize it, you're ready to bring others on board meaningfully. With a clear story in place, you've gained clarity and confidence, equipping you to start collaborating effectively.

If you have a co-founder or a small team, or if you're leading an internal project, your first step may be to collaborate with them. You can provide the story blocks, invite their input and compare their answers with yours. This ensures that you've got the story straight, you haven't missed any opportunities and you haven't inadvertently created confusion or potential conflicts.

This collaborative exercise can be valuable for team development and alignment. Imagine your team members each contributing their version of the why – this shared exploration can surface insights you hadn't considered and help shape a more unified narrative. If you feel the responsibility for the story sits primarily with you, share your version, demonstrate how it fits within the six blocks and ask if they would approach anything differently.

At this stage, your story is small and flexible, making it easy to adjust. If you share it with a co-founder or manager and hear 'That's not how we're doing it – we're doing it this way instead', or even the dreaded 'That's still being decided', this will help identify potential misalignments early on. It's far better to learn now that a director doesn't like the project name or disagrees with the timeline, rather than after a full rollout.

I've found this approach to be a healthy way to work, as it's unlikely all six blocks will provoke serious disagreement. You can kick off conversations by saying: 'We all agree on these parts. We just need to tackle this.' Consider structuring a meeting, or a series of mini-meetings, to focus on one block at a time. This keeps the focus on solving specific issues rather than descending into chaos during a meeting where the more you talk, the less clarity you have.

Collaboration

The beauty of the speed story is its ability to diagnose itself. It reveals gaps and identifies which story block needs attention. For instance, if someone insists on removing the how, you need to agree on what will replace it. If no agreement is reached, then pause, resolve the disagreement and reconstruct the story before continuing with engagement.

Your initial collaboration may go smoothly – everyone in your inner circle agrees on all six blocks, excited to have a clear way to communicate the essence of your work. However, challenges will always arise when sharing the story with a wider audience, such as stakeholders or partners. They may raise concerns or request that the story be repurposed to suit their audience. They may want more detail, or less. This is normal and part of collaboration. A speed story is built to cope with life in the real world – it's not a fixed statement that you paint onto a wall in six-foot letters but nobody reads.

This is where the adaptability of your story blocks becomes invaluable. Use the story as a compass – not to create a perfect, unchanging version, but as a guide to help you stay on track. Adjust the details when needed, ensuring your message continues to resonate while staying true to what you want to achieve for your business or project.

Examples of flexibility in action

- **Adapting the why:** For different audiences, you might focus on shared goals of growth and innovation for partners, while for customers, you may highlight delivering exceptional value. The key is ensuring all of these are logical sub-whys linked to the core why in your story. For instance, in our GrowBot story, the main why is 'to help farmers thrive despite current climate challenges'. However, when Eva speaks at a global farming conference, she may want to add a sub-why – she knows first-hand how hard this can be. Her sales manager, speaking to a significant potential client, might add another sub-why: 'to help farmers thrive despite current climate challenges using the most competitively priced solutions'.
- **Adjusting the how:** For stakeholders, this could involve explaining specific metrics and milestones, while for a broader team, it could mean simplifying the steps into more digestible actions. This adds value under a cohesive 'how arc'. Returning to our Project Change example, the how was fixed as weekly updates because the Transformation Director

Collaboration

knew that's what they could consistently commit to. But this 'how arc' can be enriched by creating a dashboard with metrics and milestones for stakeholders, which the Director can draw from for updates, or by having the project team send digestible actions for weekly meetings, which the Director can use to validate their importance with seniority.

All of this collaboration enhances the relevance and impact of what you want to achieve, and it works because it's connected to your core story. The point isn't to make the story perfect – it's to use it as a compass to guide you, ensuring the details adapt as necessary while staying aligned with your ultimate goals.

So what? Over to you…

1. Who in your immediate circle could help you refine your story? Identify key individuals – teammates, co-founders or trusted advisors who you think need to see the story or who you want to show it to.

Collaboration

2. Are there gaps in your story? Draft a message for your collaborators sharing your story or story blocks. Ask if they would change anything, and plan how and when you'll work on their feedback.

3. Who do you want to collaborate with, and in what order? Make a list of all the people you want to involve in this process or who you know will want to be included. Prioritize them to get a feel for the order in which you want to engage.

Day 10
Momentum

Congratulations – you've made it to the final day! Now that you've created, refined and tested your speed story, it's time to talk about keeping that story alive, especially during challenging times. The real magic of storytelling lies not just in telling the story once but in how it continues to evolve, adapt and energize everything that follows – even when things get tough.

Your story has already sparked interest, driven collaboration and started to build a sense of direction. Today, we'll focus on how to keep that energy alive – even when the initial novelty of the business or project has worn off and you've faced some challenges along the way. Momentum is about sustaining enthusiasm beyond the honeymoon phase, ensuring that your story keeps people engaged and motivated over time.

Momentum isn't just about maintaining forward motion – it's about keeping people motivated, even when the excitement of the early days fades and obstacles emerge. When setbacks occur, reminding your team of the progress they've made – how the story has grown and adapted – can rekindle enthusiasm.

The groundwork you've laid with these story blocks pays off particularly well in tough times. When enthusiasm dips or when you're faced with setbacks, revisiting your story can help remind everyone of the progress that's been made. You started with six simple story blocks – who, what, where, when, how and why – and now you can use them to track how far you've come, adapt as needed and show others the journey and the gains along the way. This keeps people motivated and focused, allowing your story to remain the compass that guides you all forward, even when times are challenging.

How momentum has worked for GrowBot

Let's look at how this has worked for Eva and GrowBot. They've experienced ups and downs since creating their speed story. They failed to gain traction in certain markets, and the university partnership ended when funding was cut. However, GrowBot succeeded in other markets, and the head of the university department came to lead their robot development. Now, they have a robotic system instead of just one prototype. Revisiting their story reveals how things have broadly stayed on track, helping to keep the team and investors aligned and showing how far they've come despite the obstacles.

GrowBot story blocks: then versus now

Story block	Then	Now
Who	GrowBot	GrowBot
What	A robot designed to help farmers manage their crops more efficiently	A robotic system designed to help farmers manage their crops more efficiently
Where	Used on farms struggling with irrigation	Used on farms struggling with irrigation in high-rainfall countries

Story block	Then	Now
When	Built out of founder Eva's experience as a farmer and her partnership with a university robotics lab	Built out of founder Eva's experience as a farmer and the expertise of a leading robot researcher
How	Uses sensor technology and AI to optimize crop management	Uses sensor technology and AI to optimize crop management
Why	To help farmers thrive despite current climate challenges	To help farmers thrive despite current climate challenges

If there were no story, it would be easy to get focused on what's gone wrong or feel like you're stuck in a constant state of flux. But by coming back to your story, you regain clarity and confidence.

It also reveals opportunities – like how the 'where' shows they've found a niche by focusing on high-rainfall regions. While that niche may have emerged from a setback, it positions GrowBot more effectively for those specific markets, which in turn could lead to new areas of development. For instance, perhaps GrowBot should revisit the how and consider whether the focus should be on specific types of crops instead of all crops.

The speed story acts as a guide, not to create a perfect, unchanging version of the business, but to ensure you're always on track, adapting as needed to meet challenges and opportunities head-on.

The beauty of your story

The beauty of your story is that it helps you and others see how far you've come. As setbacks arise, the story provides an opportunity to regroup, celebrate progress and adjust as needed. Use your story as a compass – not to create a perfect, unchanging version, but as a guide to help you stay on track, adjust the details and ensure your message continues to resonate while staying true to what you want to achieve for your business or project.

So what? Over to you...

1. How does your story set the foundation for long-term momentum? Reflect on each of your story blocks (who, what, where, when, how and why). Are they specific enough to provide clarity while remaining flexible enough to adapt, much like in GrowBot's journey?

2. How can you use your story to future-proof momentum? Think about what you can do now to introduce your story and embed it effectively. How will this help you sustain energy by revisiting progress and showing the bigger picture when it's most needed over the coming months and even years?

3. You now possess a powerful tool that can transform how you, your business or your project make an impact. What is the first bold action you'll take to deliver your speed storytelling? Jot down some ideas, choose your favourite and take that step today!

Conclusion

You've made it! Ten days, ten steps, and now not only are you equipped with a powerful tool – speed storytelling – but you've applied it to transform how you communicate about your current business or project.

Throughout this journey, you've seen how simple story blocks – who, what, where, when, how and why – can evolve into something much more. From sparking initial interest and fostering collaboration to sustaining long-term momentum, your story is now more than a collection of words – it has become a compass that guides action, aligns teams and inspires others.

In my experience, many businesses struggle with storytelling because they fall into common traps – using vague language, relying on jargon or overloading their stories with irrelevant details. These mistakes create barriers to engagement and diminish the impact of otherwise great ideas. By following the structured approach outlined in this book, you've learned how to avoid these pitfalls. The simplicity of the six building blocks helps you focus on what truly matters, ensuring clarity and relevance. As you've practised crafting your story in around 50 Mighty Words®, you've also built the habit of concise communication, setting you up for success in real-world interactions.

Your story is your power – make sure the world hears it. Share it boldly, refine it when necessary and use it to keep driving your vision forward. Remember, the story doesn't end here – this is just the beginning. Keep telling it, seek feedback to enhance it and watch how it continues to make an impact.

50 Mighty Words® framework

Use the six story blocks to find your story. Then, put them together to create a speed story of around 50 words that will make an impact!

- **Who (hero):** [Give your business/project name.]
- **What (action):** [Describe what it does in a brief, clear statement.]
- **Where (setting):** [State where it makes an impact, using familiar references for quick context – these can be a geographical location or a sector or a problem.]
- **When (timeline):** [Mention relevant experience, history or key trends.]
- **How (process):** [Explain how it achieves its purpose.]
- **Why (motivation):** [Clarify the reason behind it – what problem does it solve?]
- **Find out more:** [Insert your website or the one place you want people to go next.]

Example answer: [Hero] is a [description of what it does] that operates in [setting]. It was developed based on [timeline experience] and uses [how] to achieve [motivation]. Find out more at [your website].

One story, many business uses: adapting your speed storytelling blocks

Now you have your story blocks, you can start building. Designed for flexibility, these blocks help you communicate faster and more effectively across different settings. Here are some ways you can put them to work:

- **Presentations:** Open with your 50 Mighty Words® to set the stage, then dive deeper into each element. Begin with a brief overview to provide context and expand on each block in dedicated slides or sections.
- **Emails:** Use the who and what in the subject line to grab attention, and include the full 50 Mighty Words® in the body as a clear, concise introduction before adding more details.
- **Social media:** Adapt your story blocks to fit each platform's character limits. For X

(Twitter), focus on the who, what and why. For added depth on LinkedIn, expand to include how and where.
- **Website content:** Feature the 50 Mighty Words® as a tag line, opening statement or introductory paragraph on your home page, product pages or landing pages to quickly convey your core message.
- **Networking events:** Craft an 'elevator pitch' version of your 50 Mighty Words®, emphasizing the who and what while hinting at the why to spark curiosity and encourage follow-up questions.
- **Reports and proposals:** Incorporate the 50 Mighty Words® into the executive summary or introduction, giving readers a concise overview before they dive into the details.

Team-building: speed storytelling together

Now you've coached yourself on how to use the 50 Mighty Words® framework and speed storytelling for your business, why not share it all with your team to help you build a stronger story together, diagnose challenges in a neutral way and uncover insights and opportunities? Here's how to use the framework to align your team, find the positives and tackle challenges constructively:

1. **Find out how everyone answers the questions:** Start by having each team member individually answer the story block prompts – who, what, where, when, how and why – based on their understanding of the business or project. This reveals different perspectives on the core story.
2. **Bring the answers together to compare:** Share and compile everyone's answers to see where responses naturally align. Begin by

looking at the areas of agreement – these are the positives you can build on, providing a foundation of clarity and confidence. Note any differences for discussion, as these can highlight opportunities for growth.

3. **Spot opportunities, gaps and potential conflicts:** Use the combined answers to identify holes in the story, inconsistencies or areas where the team feels less confident. By separating what's working from what's not, you can maintain momentum and focus on refining specific areas rather than feeling overwhelmed.

4. **Provide a neutral process for addressing challenges:** Approach confusion or conflicts as differences in the story blocks rather than personal disagreements. This creates a collaborative problem-solving environment, allowing the team to tackle issues constructively and build a more cohesive story.

5. **Collaborate to strengthen the story:** Work together to refine the story based on your findings, using areas of alignment as a foundation. Address gaps and differing perspectives to ensure the final story is

comprehensive, consistent and embraced by the whole team.

Next steps

You might do this in one session or break it into a starter session followed by some focused follow-up sessions on the blocks where you've all discovered you want to do more thinking together. For example, the how block can reveal different approaches, providing an opportunity to discuss how to prioritize and integrate them effectively.

By using the 50 Mighty Words® framework in this way, you not only build a clear, impactful story together, but also foster shared understanding and confidence. It helps your team focus on what needs work while appreciating what's already strong, turning the process into a constructive experience.

Enjoyed this? Then you'll love…

Exposure: Insider secrets to make your business a go-to authority for journalists

** Business Book Awards 2023 Finalist **

> 'A must-read for founders. This is truly a game-changing guide.' – Eileen Burbidge MBE

Have you ever seen a competitor get great headlines and thought, 'Hey! Why wasn't that us?' Get insider secrets to find out:

- How to set your business apart and cut through the noise, using media coverage
- How to prepare your business to become a go-to authority for journalists from day one
- The end-to-end process of getting media coverage, demystified

- How to align media relations with your growth strategy and scale coverage

Included: An invaluable media relations toolkit with actionable templates, scripts and cheat sheets for transformational results

About Felicity Cowie

Who: Felicity Cowie
What: business storytelling strategist
Where: works globally
When: uses her award-winning experience as a communications troubleshooter and former BBC journalist
How: shares and embeds her 50 Mighty Words® framework
Why: to help businesses bring their best ideas to life
Find out more: www.cowiecom.com

Other 6-Minute Smarts titles

Building Great Teams (based on *Workshop Culture* by Alison Coward)

Do Change Better (based on *How to be a Change Superhero* by Lucinda Carney)

How to be Happy at Work (based on *My Job Isn't Working!* by Michael Brown)

How to Get to Know Your Customer (based on *Do Penguins Eat Peaches?* by Katie Tucker)

Mastering People Management (based on *Mission: To Manage* by Marianne Page)

No-Nonsense PR (based on *Hype Yourself* by Lucy Werner)

Present Like a Pro (based on *Executive Presentations* by Jacqui Harper)

Reimagine Your Career (based on *Work/Life Flywheel* by Ollie Henderson)

Sales Made Simple (based on *More Sales Please* by Sara Nasser Dalrymple)

The Listening Leader (based on *The Listening Shift* by Janie Van Hool)

Write to Think (based on *Exploratory Writing* by Alison Jones)

Look out for more titles coming soon! Visit www.practicalinspiration.com for all our latest titles.